Explore the World

Discoveries that shaped our world

Illustrated and written by Anton Hallmann
Translated by Ryan Eyers

LITTLE
GESTALTEN

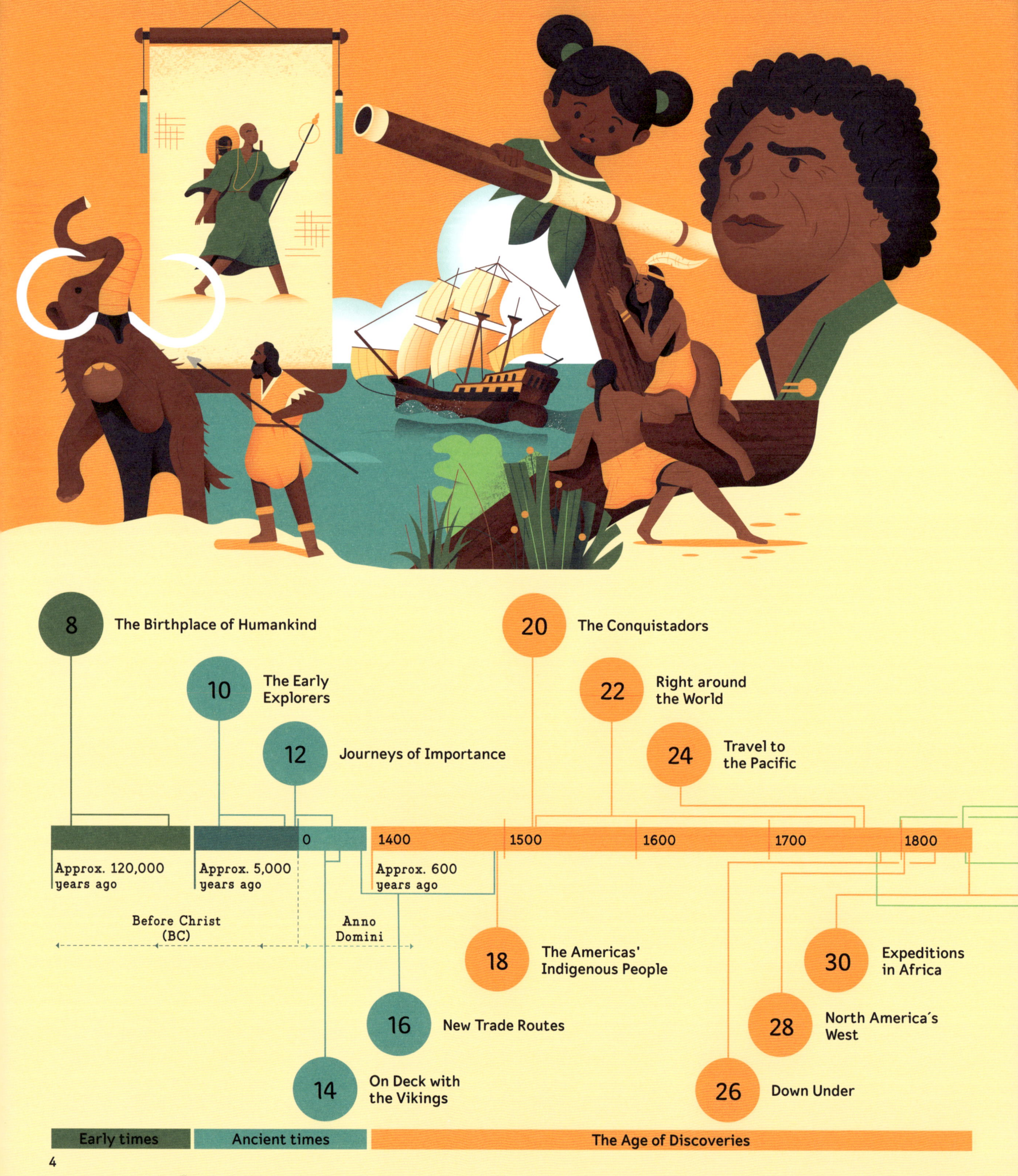

8 The Birthplace of Humankind

10 The Early Explorers

12 Journeys of Importance

20 The Conquistadors

22 Right around the World

24 Travel to the Pacific

Approx. 120,000 years ago

Approx. 5,000 years ago

Approx. 600 years ago

0 | 1400 | 1500 | 1600 | 1700 | 1800

Before Christ (BC)

Anno Domini

18 The Americas' Indigenous People

30 Expeditions in Africa

16 New Trade Routes

28 North America's West

14 On Deck with the Vikings

26 Down Under

Early times | Ancient times | The Age of Discoveries

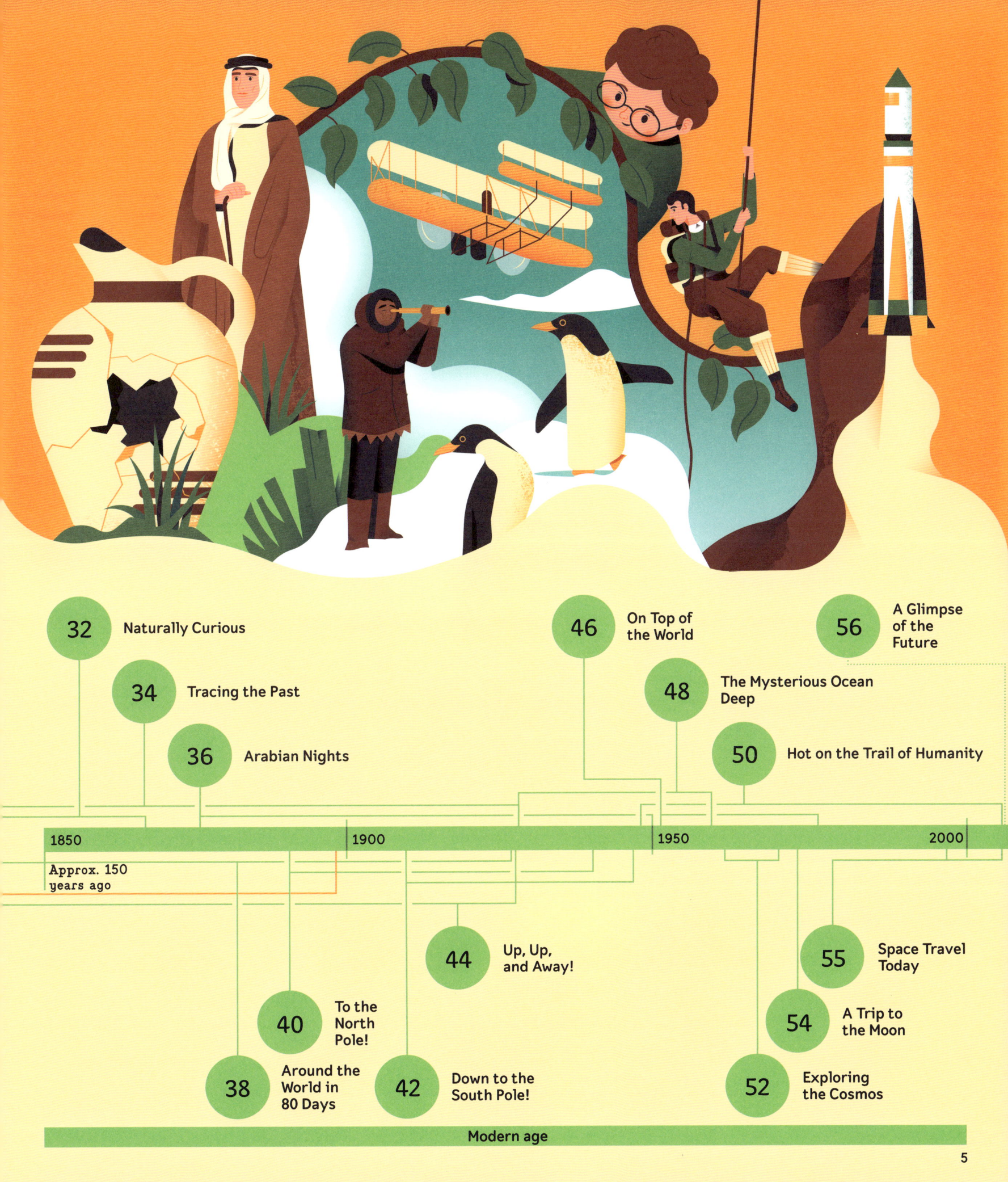

6

ADVENTURE AWAITS!

Every day, we all discover something new: it could be food that we have never tried before, an unfamiliar insect perched on a flower, a film that inspires us, or a newly opened ice-cream parlor that offers the tastiest flavors. We continue to make discoveries our entire lives—curiosity about the new and unknown makes us all explorers.

Thanks to this spirit of discovery, we now know a great deal about our planet, its plants and animals, and the many cultures. All journeys of discovery have one thing in common: they change the way we see the world. Through expeditions undertaken centuries ago, humans began to trade with each other, exchanging not only useful things but also valuable knowledge. The plants you can see from your window and the food you eat perhaps only found their way to you as a result of one of these trips.

Of course, someone who discovers a new ice-cream parlor is unlikely to be celebrated as a great explorer. History records "explorers" as those who, with the help of travel reports and maps, first describe a region for others who were not previously aware of it. This meant their audience was able to learn about the region without having to travel there themselves. However, it's worth noting that, historically, there have usually been people who did already know these places—the people who lived there. Throughout Western history, explorers have often been celebrated as heroes, but this image has begun to change in recent times, as along with the exciting new things they found, they also caused a lot of harm to the people who lived in these "discovered" regions.

Additionally, many famous expeditions and journeys were the result of great feats of teamwork, and not simply the accomplishments of individual people.

It is usually only together that we can achieve the impossible! For many years, those who assisted the explorers during their journeys of discovery were forgotten. Often, they were the indigenous people of the respective regions, whose knowledge of the landscape and its nature made it possible for the explorers to reach their intended destinations. Through the pages of this book, we get to know some of these key figures and the roles they played on certain expeditions.

Our journey will take us not only far back into the distant past and right around the world, we'll also be climbing the highest mountain on the planet and diving down into the oceans' depths. Finally, we'll even be venturing into space with a few courageous humans—and animals!

Let's strike out together and get to know the world around us. That's the only way we can understand how it works and then find our own place within it.

THE BIRTHPLACE OF HUMANKIND

The first traces of human activity were found in Africa, the starting point from which our ancestors later traveled to all four corners of the Earth. These humans were the first explorers. Here we can see the paths they took.

More than 60,000 years ago, stone spears were already being used as tools and weapons.

Leaving Africa

For a long time, humans lived only in Africa, but about 120,000 years ago they began to explore other parts of the world as well. This led to some of the most significant journeys of discovery in the history of humankind. We're still not totally sure why they started off on their wanderings, but it was probably in search of new hunting grounds or because of changes in the climate.

EUROPE

AFRICA

Imagine, how crowded it would have become in Africa if people hadn't started to travel.

Look, it's a skull of a gnu!

The First Journeys of Discovery

In the scientific world, humans are known as *Homo sapiens*, which means "wise human." Their first destinations outside Africa were the Middle East and Southeast Asia. Many thousands of years later, a second wave of humans migrated from Africa to Europe. From Asia, they eventually made it all the way down to Australia.

From Asia to America

The last major landmass to be inhabited by humans was what we now call the Americas. Researchers are still trying to figure out how exactly humans were able to get there from Asia, but one thing is certain: they reached the continent at least 15,000 years ago, either by journeying over the ice in the Far North (that is, from modern-day Russia to Alaska) or by making their way across the ocean.

Mammoths were very appealing prey for the early humans, and not only as a giant food source— the ivory from their tusks was used to make weapons.

ASIA

NORTH AMERICA

The adze was the Polynesians' most important tool, which they used for many things, including the building of canoes.

PACIFIC ISLANDS

AUSTRALIA

1500–1300 BC

Across the Pacific

The last of humankind's major and difficult first-time voyages was to Polynesia (a scattered collection of many small islands in the middle of the Pacific Ocean). The ancestors of today's Polynesians were incredibly gifted seafarers, which made it possible for them to successfully cope with very difficult sea conditions. They observed the wind, the stars, ocean currents, and the flight paths of birds to help plan their routes across the ocean.

THE EARLY EXPLORERS

After they had ventured beyond Africa, humans gradually became less nomadic. This led to the creation of the first settlements, which then became the starting points for many new journeys of discovery.

2300–1500 BC

HANNO

ca. 470 BC

Egyptian Journeys

The first written reports about such journeys that still exist date back to antiquity. The oldest-recorded explorer is the Egyptian Harchuf, who completed four long sea journeys from Egypt down to present-day Sudan and along the Red Sea. He promoted trade and friendly relations with neighboring countries such as Nubia (now a region in Sudan). The queen Hatshepsut commissioned the earliest-known exploratory expedition, to the land of Punt, which was believed to lie east of Egypt on the Mediterranean coast. More than 200 people traveled to Punt and returned with all kinds of new luxuries, such as frankincense and ebony.

At Sea!

Meet Hanno the Navigator. Hanno came from Carthage, one of the most important trading cities in northern Africa during the Ancient Mediterranean period. In about 500 BC, Hanno undertook a great sea voyage into the Atlantic and along the west coast of Africa. No one knows exactly how far he traveled; some think he made it all the way to Gabon, while others doubt he made it much further than the Canary Islands. Just as with many other accounts of ancient history, it is difficult to separate fantasy from reality when it comes to the story of Hanno—especially since the only record of his journey is his own personal account.

ASIA

PHOENICIA

CARTHAGE

EGYPT

NUBIA

PUNT

AFRICA

Alexander the Great

The figure of Alexander the Great is shrouded in legend, with some records even claiming that he was the son of Zeus. But how did he earn such fame and glory? With a brilliant military mind and an enormous army, he established the largest empire of all antiquity, which stretched from Greece to Central Asia. This made him the most powerful man of his time.

Alexander the Great is widely considered one of the most influential people in human history. While many perceive him to have been a ruthless tyrant and destroyer, the empire he forged did also result in much cultural and technological exchange and the formation of new blends of religious belief.

ca. 330 BC

What is Alexander riding away from?

Probably a cat—he was scared of them!

ALEXANDER THE GREAT

There are countless depictions of Alexander the Great, including on great murals and on vases, all of which present him as a hero.

JOURNEYS OF IMPORTANCE

Asia is the largest continent in the world, and has long been home to many different peoples, some of whom also undertook great journeys of discovery, either at the order of their ruler or because of their religious beliefs.

Zhang Qian's Travels

Beginning in about 200 BC, China was ruled by the Han dynasty (a dynasty is when a region is ruled by the same family for several generations). At this time, the Xiongnu, a horse-riding nomadic people, lived in what is now Mongolia and frequently raided the northern part of the dynasty's lands. To try to change things, the Chinese emperor sent the explorer Zhang Qian to make alliances in the north. Unfortunately, Zhang was quickly captured by the Xiongnu, who then imprisoned him for 10 years. When he was finally able to escape, he came across the nomadic Yuezhi people.

ca. 130 BC

ZHANG QIAN

I would also like to make a journey on a horse.

AREA OF THE XIONGNU

Balkh

ASIA

Chang'an

HAN DYNASTY

Zhang lived with the Yuezhi for a year and documented their daily lives and customs. His reports showed the Chinese emperor that highly developed cultures existed in the western part of the Asian continent. Although Zhang's journey had not resulted in the forging of any military alliances, it did spark the beginning of trade with the Yuezhi. Over time, this trade between the Far East and Central Asia increased dramatically, leading to the creation of the Silk Road, which was used by merchants and traders for centuries to transport goods such as horses, spices, and—above all—silk.

Once you've ridden through China you probably won't be able to sit down for a while.

Etheria's writings are mostly made up of letters that she sent to her sisters while traveling on her pilgrimage.

ETHERIA

ca. 399–412

ca. 381–384

The Spread of Religions

The Silk Road also provided a route for new ideas and religions to travel to different lands. Some of the pilgrims who traveled along the Silk Road left behind reports of their travels and encounters for us to discover, including Faxian, a Chinese Buddhist monk. Buddhism is a religion and philosophy that originally came from India. At the end of the fourth century, Faxian traveled from China to India to study Buddhism at its source and brought many Buddhist writings back to China with him. His books are full of stories about unique regional customs, as well as many Buddhist teachings and rituals.

Christians and Muslims also made pilgrimages. The Spanish Christian Etheria, for example, traveled across Egypt, Syria, and Israel in the fourth century, using the Bible as her travel guide. Her writings are the oldest-surviving travelogues that we know of.

The Muslim Ahmad ibn Fadlan was a scholar from Arabia who traveled to the region surrounding the River Volga (present-day Russia). His account of his travels is very detailed, recording everything from the clothing of those he met to the unique features of the buildings he came across. Ibn Fadlan is believed to have been instrumental in bringing Islam to the region.

IBN FADLAN

ca. 922

ON DECK WITH THE VIKINGS

Because of the terror they inspired for so many years, the Vikings generally get a pretty bad rap in the history books. Their marauding took them to the farthest corners of the Earth, but they returned with much more than what they had looted.

Viking Life

The Vikings were a collection of peoples from Scandinavia, the northernmost part of Europe. Life there was very hard because the cold climate made it difficult to work the land. For this reason, its inhabitants decided to set off in search of more fertile land.

As they journeyed, the Vikings attacked many settlements on land as well as ships at sea. They were incredible shipbuilders, and these were their most dangerous weapons: their longships were lightning-fast and very nimble. But the Vikings were not only warriors, they were also collectors of stories and knowledge, creating a rich culture over the course of their travels.

Can I trade Louis for this axe?

This shield would look awesome in my room!

Alongside their famous longships, the Vikings also used ships called *knarrs* to transport cargo.

The Vikings' weapons were not only used for carrying out raids, they were also traded with coastal Europeans for honey, spices, and even different metals.

ca. 980

Erik the Red

The Viking Erik the Red was so named because of his striking red hair and beard, but he soon lived up to the promise of his name by getting plenty of blood on his hands. After committing murder, he was exiled from Iceland, which led him to set off toward Greenland (an island east of North America that is in fact the world's largest). Once here, he established its first European settlement.

Off to America

Erik the Red's son Leif Eriksson was born in Greenland. Eriksson heard stories about an undiscovered land farther off to the west—modern-day North America—where the grass was a lush green, the rivers were full of salmon, and apparently even grapevines grew. After setting off in search of this place, eventually reaching what is now Newfoundland, Eriksson named it Vinland (Wineland), in honor of its grapevines.

GREENLAND

ICELAND

1002

Leif's route

Erik's route

In about 980, Erik the Red journeyed from Iceland to Greenland; some years later (about 1002), his son Leif would make it all the way to North America.

NEWFOUNDLAND

LEIF ERIKSSON

With Eriksson's help, Icelander Gudrid Thorbjarnardóttir also traveled to Newfoundland via Greenland. She is considered the first European to have given birth in the Americas. After returning to Iceland, Thorbjarnardóttir was led by her thirst for adventure to make a pilgrimage to Rome. She is documented as one of the most widely traveled women of the Middle Ages.

ca. 1000

GUDRID THORBJARNARDÓTTIR

NEW TRADE ROUTES

In the thirteenth and fourteenth centuries, many people undertook trade expeditions across Asia, North Africa, and Europe. Some of these travelers documented their journeys, collecting knowledge about a range of cultures along the way.

Whether by foot, on the back of a camel, or by ship, products have been transported from one place to another in large quantities for thousands of years. Despite the large number of people traveling around during the late medieval period, only a few reports remain of their journeys. Thankfully, the likes of Ibn Battuta, Marco Polo, and Zheng He documented their travels. These three figures all came from very different parts of the world.

Tlemcen

Tunis

I know the way!

Baghdad

Jerusalem

Ibn Battuta

Ibn Battuta was from northern Africa, and began his travels aged 21. During his lifetime, he traveled 72,700 miles (117,000 kilometers) through northern Africa and the Arabian Peninsula, and all the way to China—the equivalent of circling the globe three times!

1325–1354

In 1334, Ibn Battuta arrived in Delhi, now the capital of India.

Zeila

IBN BATTUTA

Mogadishu

By Land

The Silk Road was a giant network of trade routes that connected East Asia and the Mediterranean. It was used for transporting spices, fabrics, and porcelain.

The Silk Road was a dangerous route, so people tended to protect themselves by traveling in large groups.

Marco Polo

Despite receiving large quantities of goods from China, Europeans knew very little about this giant empire. This all changed when the Italian Marco Polo returned from his 24-year exploration of the Far East. Despite the length of his travels, his reports make no mention of Chinese tea ceremonies or of the letterpress. This has led many to believe that he was never actually there.

MARCO POLO

1271–1295

Peking

Yangzhou

Hangzhou

Quanzhou

1405–1433

Delhi

Khambhat

Honnavar

Calicut

Zheng He's fleet was enormous, comprising 300 ships and up to 30,000 troops. His expeditions redirected a large quantity of trade from the Silk Road to sea routes.

ZHENG HE

Zheng He

China wanted to advertise and sell its valuable products to the rest of the world. This was the reason behind Admiral Zheng He being sent off with a fleet of merchant ships. During his seven expeditions, he traveled to many far-flung locations, including the Indian subcontinent, the Middle East, and even East Africa. On these journeys, he traded tea, silk, and porcelain for pearls, cinnamon, and precious stones.

Ha, I already drew the best route on the map!

1487–1488

Dias's route

Da Gama's route

1497–1499

To India by Sea

There were many checkpoints on the Silk Road where guards demanded a fee from those who wished to continue their journey. This led the Portuguese to search for a cheaper trade route. On the hunt for a way to Asia by sea, Bartolomeu Dias was the first European to sail around the southernmost tip of Africa, with navigator Vasco da Gama later making it all the way to India. Now Europeans could trade with Asian peoples without first having to traverse the entire Middle East. But because this new route was still very long, the search for alternatives continued.

THE AMERICAS' INDIGENOUS PEOPLES

By the time of the Age of Discovery, almost the entire world had been settled by humans. If an expedition reached new territory, its members often came into conflict with the people who already lived there. An example of the consequences of these expeditions is the "discovery" of the Americas.

Before the Arrival of Columbus

Before the Italian navigator Christopher Columbus accidentally landed in the Americas in 1492 while searching for a new sea route to Asia, many hundreds of indigenous groups lived throughout the two continents. Each had their own customs and rituals, and many of these cultures were highly concentrated and organized, living on farms or in cities, while others were nomadic peoples who were consistently on the move.

Because the Vikings' records of Vinland had been lost, Europeans were unaware of the existence of the Americas. For this reason, Columbus was long celebrated as the discoverer of the dual continents. Of course, neither the Vikings nor Columbus "discovered" the continents, as people had already been living there for 15,000 years. For the indigenous peoples of the Americas, Columbus's arrival marked the start of a terrible era of suffering.

Cahokia was North America's biggest city before Columbus's arrival. It was located near the Mississippi River and existed from 700 to 1300.

Other Visitors

The West African king Abu Bakr II counts among those from abroad who may have landed in the Americas before Columbus. He is said to have arrived as early as the end of the fourteenth century and spread African culture among the local people he met, although there is no clear evidence that proves this actually took place.

The Polynesians, masters of boatbuilding, may also have reached the Americas earlier than the Italian explorer. A thousand years ago, the sweet potato became a key part of their diet, although it had only previously existed in South America. While the Vikings were building their houses way up north, it is believed that either the Polynesians traveled to South America or indigenous peoples from South America made it all the way to Polynesia. How exactly that could have happened remains a mystery.

Sweet potatoes! I am so glad that South America was discovered!

The Indigenous Americans and Columbus

When Columbus arrived in the Caribbean, he encountered the Taíno people, who lived in small villages, grew grains, produced gold jewelry, and were considered a peace-loving people. At their first meeting with Columbus, they exchanged cotton for glass beads. When Columbus returned on his second voyage, he began to enslave and murder the indigenous peoples of the Caribbean. Even the Spanish Crown, under whose commission Columbus was traveling, did not approve of these actions, as they saw the local people as possible converts to Christianity. Many of them were violently forced to accept a religion that was not theirs.

Columbus probably died still thinking that he had found the western sea route to India, but this was disproved by the Italian explorer Amerigo Vespucci a few years later. He realized that Columbus had in fact come across a whole new landmass previously unknown to Europeans, one that now bears Vespucci's name.

AMERIGO VESPUCCI

1497–1504

Hopefully no one got seasick … Which route would I have chosen?

Lisbon

Columbus's route

Vespucci's route

AFRICA

SOUTH AMERICA

1492–1504

CHRISTOPHER COLUMBUS

Initially, Columbus traded goods and food with the indigenous Caribbeans, but from the outset he had plans to enslave them.

THE CONQUISTADORS

Following Columbus's sea voyages, many more campaigns of conquest set out in the name of the Spanish Crown, largely in the direction of Central and South America. This had a devastating effect on the indigenous peoples of these lands, with many of their populations decimated as a result of Spanish colonization.

Greedy for Gold

The journeys were called *conquista* (the Spanish word for "conquest") and the Spaniards who undertook them, *conquistadors* (meaning "conquerors"). Their main goal was to capture new territory, secure and extract resources, and steal as much gold as possible. Central and South America were populated with large cities that contained many treasures. This led to the indigenous peoples experiencing raids and looting at the hands of the Spanish, who were prepared to sacrifice a great deal of human life to satisfy their lust for gold.

HERNÁN CORTÉS

1521

The Downfall of the Aztecs

In the sixteenth century, the region that is now Mexico was ruled by the Aztecs, a highly developed people whose ruler during this period was Moctezuma II. Because he actively oppressed other local peoples and practiced slavery, the conquistadors were able to form alliances with those who suffered under Aztec rule. One particularly famous slave was known as La Malinche, who originally came from a noble family. She acted as a translator for conquistador Hernán Cortés and also became his lover. Her assistance was crucial in helping Cortés overthrow and destroy the Aztec Empire.

LA MALINCHE

The Incas and Francisco Pizarro

The Inca Empire spread out across the western part of South America. Incas were famous for their cities in the mountains, their trade routes, and their farming skills in high mountain regions, but the Spaniard Francisco Pizarro had no interest in Incan culture, only their gold. On his first trip through its territory, he saw the wealth the empire possessed and resolved to conquer it. It was during the conquistador's third and final expedition, in 1532, that the fate of the Incas, their empire, and the lives of many of their people was sealed.

1533

FRANCISCO PIZARRO

GULF OF MEXICO

Cortés's route

Santiago de Cuba

Trujillo

Louis, that's not yours!

CARIBBEAN SEA

Panama

Tumbes

But I look so handsome with it on!

Pizarro's route

PACIFIC OCEAN

SOUTH AMERICA

Just like the Aztecs, the Incas had used brutal methods to acquire their wealth. This meant that they had many enemies willing to help the Spanish.

Previously, there had been two Incan brothers who both wanted to sit on the empire's throne. Eventually they went to war with each other, which weakened the entire empire. One of the brothers died in the war, while Pizarro initially presented himself to the other, Atahualpa, as an ally, with the aim of later overthrowing him.

21

RIGHT AROUND THE WORLD

The hunt for a faster route to Asia continued well after Columbus and Vespucci's travels, because it was in this part of the world that a small cluster of islands existed that were the only source for the valuable spices nutmeg and cloves.

Ferdinand Magellan

In earlier times, nutmeg and cloves were literally worth their weight in gold, and therefore promised great riches. It was precisely the promise of such riches that motivated Ferdinand Magellan to set sail in 1519 with five ships on behalf of the Spanish Crown. Magellan himself was Portuguese and an experienced sailor. The journey round the southernmost point of South America is a particularly difficult one, and one of Magellan's ships was wrecked because of dangerous storms and huge swells. The remaining fleet eventually reached the Pacific Ocean but many sailors had become ill due to the lack of food. After sailing for three months around the giant Pacific Ocean, they finally reached the Philippines.

1519–1522

Initial encounters with the indigenous peoples of the Philippines were peaceful. Conversations were led by Enrique, Magellan's slave, who was originally from the region but had been forcibly taken back to Europe. If, as the story surrounding Enrique implies, he indeed came from the Philippines, that would have made him the first person to circumnavigate the globe. It is more likely, however, that he was from Malaysia, a peninsula further to the west. His language skills and general abilities made him indispensable to Magellan.

ENRIQUE

In the late 1760s, the naturalist Jeanne Baret became the first woman to circumnavigate the globe. At the time, women were not allowed to work on ships, so Baret had to disguise herself as a man in order to get on board.

1766–1769

JEANNE BARET

A Long Sea Voyage

Magellan's attempts to claim the Philippines for Spain led to conflict. The Filipino tribal chief Lapu-Lapu was able to defeat the Spanish in battle, and Magellan was mortally wounded by a poisoned spear in the process. Command of the expedition was eventually taken over by ship captain Juan Sebastián Elcano, after what remained of Magellan's fleet reached the so-called Spice Islands (the Moluccas, now part of Indonesia); just one of the ships returned to Spain, thus completing the first circumnavigation of the globe. Although Magellan was celebrated in Spain for his exploits, in the Philippines it is Lapu-Lapu who is considered a hero.

Conditions on these ships were dire. It was cold, food was scarce, and brutal ship captains often tormented their crew.

Because fresh food spoiled too quickly, rations often consisted of hard crackers and dried meat, which kept for longer but were not very nutritious.

With fresh fruit off the menu, many sailors suffered from a lack of vitamins, leading to diseases such as scurvy. It was not until 1753 that citrus juice was recognized as being a preventative.

TRAVEL TO THE PACIFIC

Even after they had circumnavigated the planet, Europeans knew little about the contents of the Pacific. This prompted a new wave of mariners to set out to explore the largest ocean of the world in more detail.

The Search for Australia

In 1768, the British explorer and Royal Navy captain James Cook sailed across the Pacific. In Europe, there had long been the belief that one last great landmass must exist in the southern hemisphere, leading to many expeditions in search of it. Cook was an exceptional navigator and was able to chart a course simply by using the wind and the stars. He also acquired local help in the form of Tahitian navigator Tupaia, who—in contrast to the Europeans—was quite at home on Pacific waters.

1768

TUPAIA

JAMES COOK

I found New Zealand!

PACIFIC OCEAN

AUSTRALIA

Sydney

NEW ZEALAND

In 1770, Cook circumnavigated New Zealand, after which he sailed up the east coast of Australia.

HMS Endeavour

For the long journey to Australia, a coal transporter was converted and re-christened the Endeavour. With Tupaia's help, Cook was able to locate the landmass in the southern hemisphere that we now know as Australia (which comes from the Latin phrase *terra australis incognita*, or "unknown southern land").

A Map of the World

As early as the Stone Age, humans started making crude drawings to help them to return to new locations, and the first proper maps began to appear during antiquity. This led to the development of cartography, which deals with the production of land and sea maps. The invention of the letterpress made it easier for maps to be reproduced, which sped up advances in cartography and meant that maps could be updated to reflect new knowledge.

I'll put it on our globe!

Map-making also became a more unified practice, meaning maps looked similar regardless of who was producing them. Nowadays, they can be extremely precise, and the blank spaces that previously occupied some have all been filled in with illustrative detail.

Further Discoveries

Tupaia and Cook mapped the entire coastline of New Zealand. On a later expedition, Cook came across the islands of Hawaii. As was inevitably the case on such journeys, this eventually led to conflict between the local inhabitants and the seafarers. One such encounter would prove to be Cook's downfall: during a dispute with Hawaiians, while Cook was attempting to kidnap their king, he was struck on the head and then stabbed to death.

The indigenous people of New Zealand are known as Māori, and originally came from Polynesia.

Look at the two main islands of New Zealand—what do they look like to you? Like the Vikings, the Māori were also great at telling stories, which they used to explain the world around them. A major figure in many Māori myths is Māui, a trickster demigod. In one such myth, Māui and his brothers go out fishing with their canoe using a magic jawbone for a hook. They ended up with quite a catch: the North Island of New Zealand, which in Māori is known as Te Ika a Māui (Māui's fish). Similarly, one Māori name among others for the South Island is Te Waka a Māui (Māui's canoe).

DOWN UNDER

Australia is one of the southernmost landmasses in the world. This is why many still refer to it as Down Under. After James Cook landed on the east coast, the British Crown claimed the land as its own, but still needed the help of the indigenous people to explore its interior.

I feel the didgeridoo in my tummy.

The Indigenous Peoples of Australia

Australia was first settled by Aboriginal Australians 50,000 years ago. To their way of thinking, everything in nature is interconnected—plants, animals, and people. They shared their knowledge with each other through music, dance, and illustration, but did not have a system of writing.

Bungaree

Bungaree was the first Aboriginal Australian to circumnavigate Australia and took part in mapping the great landmass. He got along well with Europeans, even though he did not speak their languages.

BUNGAREE

The Hunt for Fresh Water

Following Cook's first landing on Australian soil, part of the continent became a British colony. Over time, more and more of the Australian coast was colonized by British subjects and further expeditions undertaken into the continent's interior. Captain Charles Sturt followed the paths of rivers inland in search of fresh-water reserves. He made it almost as far as the center of Australia, but found only desert. Desperate to find water and food, Sturt and his crew came across a camp of Aboriginal Australians who came to their rescue. Unlike most other settlers, Sturt never used violence against the local people.

CHARLES STURT

Edward John Eyre and Wylie

Another noteworthy duo associated with early expeditions in Australia were the British researcher Edward John Eyre and Aboriginal Australian Wylie. They traversed the continent along its southern coast. When they began to run low on supplies, Wylie knew where they could find animals to hunt. Despite the difficult conditions, they continued their journey for more than another month, in order to reach the west. All Europeans were dependent on the help of Aboriginal Australians like Wylie or Bungaree on journeys like this—without their assistance, it would have been impossible to successfully explore such a giant and barren landmass. Although they contributed to the development of much of the country, they were rarely recognized in official history books, and to this day their crucial role is not given the attention it deserves.

1840–1841

WYLIE

EDWARD JOHN EYRE

The Displacement of Aboriginal Australians

The discovery of gold in Australia in 1851 led to the arrival of a good deal more European settlers in search of a new life. Many Aboriginal Australians were forcibly removed from their homes and lands; some fled into the outback, while others tried to live among the new white arrivals. The colonizers also brought new diseases with them to the continent, to which Aboriginal Australians were not immune, leading to further loss of life on a large scale, and many died under the new colonial government or because of the newly arrived settlers.

And I can feel it in my head!

Franklin fought strongly for women's rights and their access to education.

LADY JANE FRANKLIN

from 1839

Explorer and Feminist

In the early-nineteenth century, at a time when women were restricted to the tasks of child-raising and housekeeping, the Englishwoman Lady Jane Franklin traveled along Australia's east coast. A tireless adventurer, she also traveled to Tasmania, Japan, India, and North America.

NORTH AMERICA'S WEST

Starting in the seventeenth century, the British began to colonize the east coast of North America. The west of the country remained an unknown land to the white settlers, but this would soon change.

The War for Independence

The people living in the North American colonies wanted to found their own independent country and no longer be governed by the British Crown. This is why they wrote the Declaration of Independence. Following the American Revolutionary War, the British recognized the 13 existing states as independent. This document freed the country we now know as the United States of America from British control. The regions occupied by the indigenous peoples of North America were treated as separate countries—for now, at least.

1776

Although the Declaration of Independence famously declared that "all men are created equal," it also categorized the indigenous peoples of the continent as enemies.

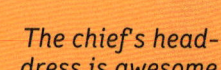
The chief's head-dress is awesome.

A New Plan

President Thomas Jefferson (in office from 1801 to 1809) wanted to expand the country's territory in the west. The indigenous tribes living there were to adapt to the lifestyles of the settlers. A key first step in this plan of westward expansion was the Louisiana Purchase of 1803, through which the United States of America "purchased" a large amount of land previously controlled by the Kingdom of France. One year later, the first expedition set off to explore this new territory.

OREGON COUNTY

SACAGAWEA

NORTH AMERICA

MERIWETHER LEWIS

1804–1806

WILLIAM CLARK

Why were the settlers so mean? The indigenous tribes were there before them.

The Lewis and Clark Expedition

This first expedition out west was led by Meriwether Lewis and his partner William Clark. For large parts of their journey they were accompanied by Sacagawea, a woman from the Lemhi Shoshone tribe, who helped them speak with other indigenous tribes they encountered. Without the assistance of many Native American peoples, the expedition would not have succeeded in its journey west. The expedition paved the way for the further settlement of North America by Europeans—and the violent suppression of indigenous peoples and their culture.

The settlers killed so many buffalo as they advanced that they almost hunted them to extinction.

The newly founded United States of America claimed the land documented by its explorers as its own. Many Native American tribes were forcibly displaced or even enslaved.

Many Native Americans also died from diseases carried into their lands by the white colonizers.

EXPEDITIONS IN AFRICA

European maps documenting the coastline of the African continent existed as early as the fifteenth century. Because of a strong focus on trade with America, European powers paid little attention to Africa for many years.

Lost Knowledge

In the Middle Ages, Africa was governed by powerful kingdoms and complex trade networks. Over the course of the next few centuries, Europeans colonized large parts of Africa's coast by violently conquering preexisting countries. This led to the loss of much knowledge of African history and the continent's rich cultural heritage.

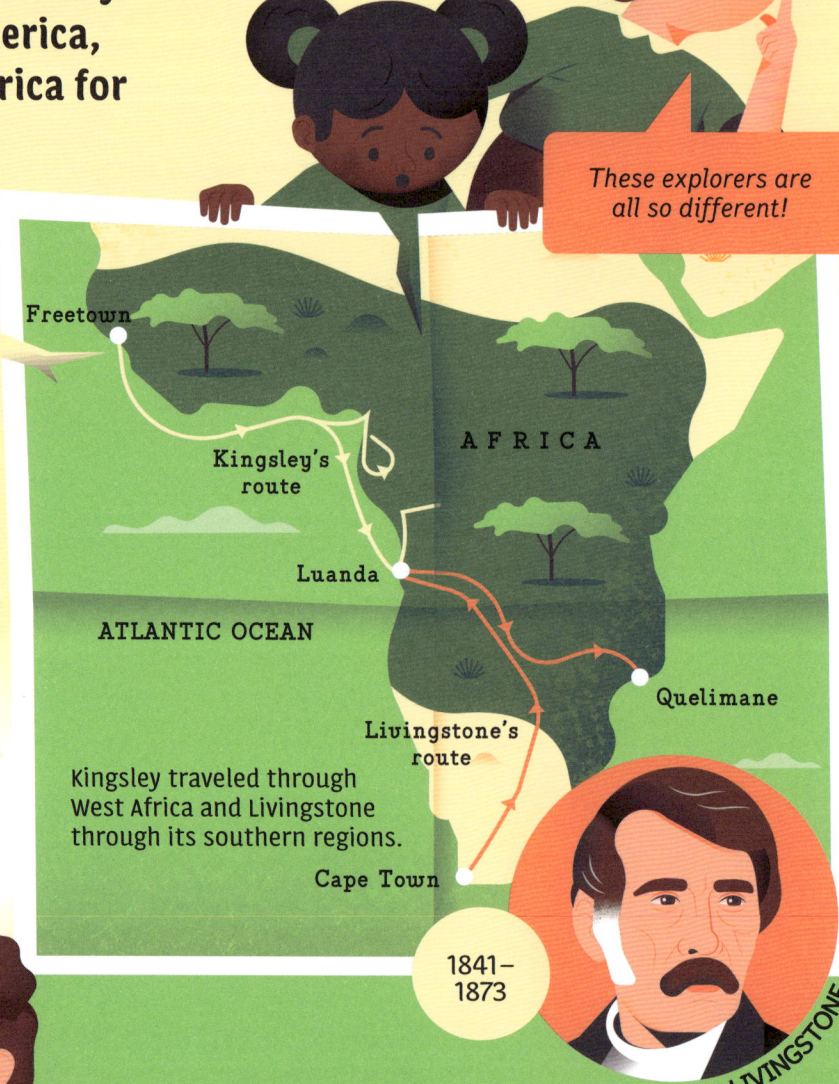

These explorers are all so different!

Freetown
Kingsley's route
A F R I C A
Luanda
ATLANTIC OCEAN
Quelimane
Livingstone's route
Kingsley traveled through West Africa and Livingstone through its southern regions.
Cape Town
1841–1873
DAVID LIVINGSTONE

Sometimes very small animals can be more dangerous than larger ones: in 1844, Livingstone survived being attacked by a lion, but in 1873 he died from malaria, a disease transmitted by mosquitoes.

David Livingstone

Scotsman David Livingstone was interested in obtaining this knowledge. He investigated the southern part of the continent and traversed it from west to east. This made him a very famous expert on Africa. Among other things, Livingstone sought to put an end to the inter-African slave trade. After one expedition he never returned and remained missing for several years, before eventually being found by Henry Morton Stanley, a journalist. By this time, Livingstone had become so weakened by malaria that he could not return to Scotland—and nor did he want to, saying that his heart belonged to Africa.

In Kingsley's time, it was uncommon for women to travel on their own.

MARY KINGSLEY

1893–1895

Mary Kingsley

Englishwoman Mary Kingsley played a major role in the European exploration of Africa in the late-nineteenth century. In Nigeria she lived with the local people and tried to stop attempts by European missionaries to convert Africans to Christianity. On her return to Europe, she brought with her many unknown fish species, a new kind of snake, and eight new kinds of insect that she had collected on her expeditions.

The Slave Trade

The practice of keeping slaves is as old as humanity itself. Slaves are people who are considered the "property" of others and therefore have no rights of their own. The colonization of North America led to the slave trade reaching a horrific new low. More and more people were captured and transported from Africa to North America to work as slaves. It took a long time for slavery to finally be abolished. It was first made illegal in the U.S. in 1865.

Slaves were often forced to exist in inhumane living conditions. Brutal punishment was common.

Slaves usually worked the land or in the home.

NATURALLY CURIOUS

Many people recognized that the real wealth obtained on expeditions came not in the form of gold but, rather, in the knowledge gathered about new plants and animals.

Charles Darwin

These new explorers wanted to discover nature and and find out more about all the plants and animals they found in these previously unknown lands. In the process of studying them, they changed our understanding of the natural world. British naturalist Charles Darwin made an astounding discovery on the Galapagos Islands.

CHARLES DARWIN

1831–1836

Darwin had so many birds ...

He observed that species had changed over the course of time and adapted to their environment. These observations inspired his theory of evolution, which explains how animals and plants had changed throughout time to become what we know now.

Large ground finch

Medium ground finch

Small tree finch

Green warbler finch

Over the course of his travels, Darwin collected thousands of samples, filled 15 notebooks with his observations, and produced about 300 illustrations.

The closely related species of Darwin's finches all share a common ancestor but, over time, developed different beaks.

If I find a new animal that no one knows about yet, I'll call it Emmaria Helouis!

Alfred Wallace

Another British naturalist, Alfred Wallace, explored South America in the mid-nineteenth century. Unfortunately he lost everything he had collected on his return journey to England due to a fire on his ship. He did not allow this to discourage him, however, and later put together another collection in East Asia. Independently of Darwin, he also developed a theory of evolution.

Wallace primarily observed birds and was the first to document many of them, including the standardwing bird-of-paradise.

1848–1862

ALFRED WALLACE

1799–1804

Alexander von Humboldt

Both Darwin and Wallace were inspired to set out on their journeys by Alexander von Humboldt, a German explorer and naturalist who had a very strong influence on the development of the natural sciences. Von Humboldt also catalogued thousands of animal and plant species in South America with the assistance of the French botanist Aimé Bonpland. In addition, he studied rocks, traversed the rain forest, climbed volcanoes, and followed rivers to their sources. Nature and its study were his life's passions.

ALEXANDER VON HUMBOLDT

TRACING THE PAST

These are old huts. You can find many things above and under them.

The search for old cities and objects has uncovered vast amounts of knowledge about how people in the distant past lived.

Archaeologists study the cultural development of humanity. Through their underground excavations, they find the remains of cultures that are sometimes thousands of years old. Although the practice of studying old objects has existed since the Middle Ages, archaeology first became a proper scientific discipline in the nineteenth century. Previously, objects had usually been uncovered by treasure hunters or grave robbers.

JOHN LLOYD STEPHENS

1839–1840

John Lloyd Stephens

American archaeology enthusiast John Lloyd Stephens was captivated by Alexander von Humboldt's descriptions of ruins in South America and came to the conclusion that there must be many more that had been swallowed up by the jungle. And he was right! On his first expedition he discovered several important Mayan cities across the continent.

1881–1888

John Wesley Gilbert was the first African-American archaeologist. His fluency in Greek meant he was able to take part in many excavations in Greece.

JOHN WESLEY GILBERT

Jane Dieulafoy

Frenchwoman Jane Dieulafoy was one of the first female archaeologists and led archaeological digs at many historic sites in Arabia. She wanted to show that women were capable of doing anything at least as well as their male counterparts, even if they were not permitted to do so.

Machu Picchu

Hiram Bingham III, an American explorer, was greatly interested in the Incas. He wanted to find their last place of refuge from the Spanish: Vilcabamba. The indigenous peoples of Peru spoke of a "lost city" situated on a ridge of hills. A farmer led Bingham to an old city that turned out to be one of the most important ruins of the Inca civilization. It was not until some years later, however, that it became clear that Bingham had not in fact come across Vilcabamba, but rather Machu Picchu. He made the ruins famous around the world and brought more than 40,000 artifacts that he had wrongfully taken back with him on his return journey, including pottery and human bones. These have only recently been returned to the nation of Peru.

1911–1913

As a woman living during the turn of the twentieth century, Harriet Boyd Hawes, an American, was not allowed to participate in archaeological expeditions. Undeterred, she took matters into her own hands and, in the process, became one of the pioneers of archaeology.

HARRIET BOYD HAWES

HOWARD CARTER

1922

Tutankhamen's Tomb

Archaeologist Howard Carter, a longtime student of Egyptian culture and history, had been searching for King Tutankhamen's tomb for many years. At the point when he was about to give up on his mission, he thought to himself: "Just one more dig." And it was precisely then, after a local boy accidentally stumbled across a stairwell, that he discovered the entrance to the tomb—a site that had remained virtually untouched since the tomb was sealed. Imagine!

Carter was extremely thorough in his search and recorded every detail, no matter how minor, in his notebooks.

ARABIAN NIGHTS

The Arabian Peninsula, which lies between Africa and Asia, has fascinated European travelers since time immemorial, but for a long period many regions there could only be entered by Muslims.

I can tell stories like Scheherazade in One Thousand and One Nights!

Mysterious Arabia

Cities such as Medina and Mecca, both in Saudi Arabia, were (and largely still are) only accessible to Muslims due to their sacred importance in the Islamic faith. As reports about these places were rare, Europeans didn't know much about them. Little by little, writings from the Middle East made their way to Europe, including those of Ibn Battuta, who painted a very romantic portrait of Arabia. Subsequently, many Europeans wanted to see the peninsula for themselves.

ANNE BLUNT

Today, almost all purebred Arabian horses can trace their lineage back to Anne Blunt's stud.

1878–1879

And I can drink a thousand and one lemonades.

Anne Blunt

The English couple Anne and Wilfrid Blunt were not only drawn to the region, but also its horses, as Anne had a stud farm (where horses are bred). She learned Arabic and befriended the Bedouins, nomadic people who live in the Arabian Desert.

Freya Stark

One book had a particularly strong effect on the writer Freya Stark: the story collection known as *Arabian Nights* or *One Thousand and One Nights*. She was given it for her ninth birthday and began to dream of travel—and what a journey they would inspire! She was one of the first non-Arabian travelers to journey by camel across the Rub' al Khali, a giant desert on the Arabian Peninsula—and the largest sand desert on Earth. She recorded her experiences in more than 20 books.

1927–1979

1945–1950

WILFRED THESIGER

Wilfred Thesiger

The British explorer Wilfred Thesiger was stationed in northern Africa during the Second World War. While waiting for the airplane that would take him back home, he received an offer to explore Arabia and describe what he saw. And that is exactly what he did! He was the first to completely traverse the Rub' al Khali.

GERTRUDE BELL

1892–1913

Gertrude Bell

Englishwoman Gertrude Bell was admired by numerous Arabian tribes for her incredible courage. She explored many regions that had previously never been visited by anyone from Europe or America, such as Syria and Saudi Arabia.

AROUND THE WORLD IN 80 DAYS

After the first successful circumnavigation of the Earth by ship in the early-sixteenth century, interest in undertaking similar journeys faded for a long time. This all changed with the publication of a particular book!

A Novel Gives the Starting Signal

When the book *Around the World in Eighty Days* by Jules Verne was published in 1872, many people were once again seized by the thrill of adventure. Phileas Fogg, the novel's globe-encircling protagonist, inspired many readers, and some were even driven to undertake their own circumnavigations—on foot, by bicycle, and by car.

THOMAS STEVENS

1884–1886

Stevens traveled the world by bicycle for two and a half years.

Wow! Around the world on a bicycle.

IDA PFEIFFER

1842–1855

By Bike and Foot

The first circumnavigation of the globe on a bicycle was achieved in the late-nineteenth century by Briton Thomas Stevens. Back then, bicycles were a relative novelty, which meant that wherever Stevens went, people wanted to see him demonstrate how his bicycle, a penny-farthing, worked.

In contrast, just a few decades earlier, Austrian Ida Pfeiffer made her journey—twice—on foot and by other means of transport. Along with her other travels, it is estimated that, in her lifetime, she traveled more than 149,000 miles (240,000 kilometers) by ship and 20,000 miles (32,000 kilometers) across land—a distance equal to seven journeys around the Earth! She recorded her experiences in books that continue to be widely read to this day.

By Airplane

Two American airplanes managed to circumnavigate the globe in 1924. Five years later, the same feat was achieved by the Graf Zeppelin. In 2016, Bertrand Piccard and André Borschberg completed the first solar-powered flight around the world.

Piccard and Borschberg had to compete their circumnavigation by solar airplane in several stages—it took them a total of 16 months.

NELLIE BLY

1889–1890

Nellie Bly in the News

In 1888, the newspaper journalist Nellie Bly presented her editor with a proposition: she wanted to undertake a trip round the world and surpass the fictional record set by Phileas Fogg in *Around the World in Eighty Days*. Her boss rejected her idea since she was a woman and would need a guardian. Bly saw things rather differently, and, a year later, set off on her journey accompanied by only a travel bag. She managed to circumnavigate the globe in 72 days—a record at the time and a sensational story for her newspaper!

CLÄRENORE STINNES

The one with the car was only a tiny bit faster.

1927–1929

By Car

The first circumnavigation of the world achieved from behind the wheel of a car was made by the female German race driver Clärenore Stinnes, who was accompanied by the Swedish photographer Carl-Axel Söderström. What was most incredible about this trip was that, at the time, there were hardly any suitable roads, meaning they often had to drive through mud and grassy fields. They often got stuck but managed to finish the trip in just over two years!

TO THE NORTH POLE!

While the majority of the planet had been explored by the nineteenth century, the Arctic remained a large, mysterious, and very white blank spot on the world map.

The Inuit were the first to explore the Arctic. They had already been surveying the region for thousands of years before the first Europeans reached the north pole. One legendary Inuit explorer was Nukapinguaq. He accompanied several European expeditions and helped researchers survive the extreme conditions.

Fridtjof Nansen

Due to the extreme cold and long, dark winters in the Arctic, early expeditions to the north pole were very dangerous. Fridtjof Nansen was from Norway and therefore at least accustomed to the cold. In Greenland he became friendly with the local Inuit peoples, who equipped him with suitable clothing and their primary means of transportation, the dogsled. Thus, Nansen learned the best way to reach the north pole.

NUKAPINGUAQ

Finally there's some snow!

1893–1896

FRIDTJOF NANSEN

A Near Miss

Nansen set off from Norway in his ship, the Fram (which means "forward" in Norwegian). He hoped to be carried to the north pole by the natural movements of the ice floes. Unfortunately, this didn't work, and the ship and its crew remained stuck in the ice. Eighteen months later, Nansen finally set off on skis and dogsleds and reached a point very far north, but not quite the north pole.

1908–1909

The Arctic is huge from above.

Amundsen's route

The First at the North Pole

Many failed attempts preceded the journey taken by Americans Robert Peary and Matthew Henson with the assistance of four Inuits—Ooqeah, Ootah, Egingwah, and Seeglo—during which they supposedly reached the north pole. Many researchers are skeptical that the expedition actually did make it as far as that, as the duration of their journey appears too short for it to have been possible. Peary's Arctic-research findings are considered to be of significant value, however.

1926

Polar researcher Roald Amundsen flew over the north pole in a zeppelin.

Nansen's route

North pole

Peary and Henson's route

ROBERT PEARY

GREENLAND

MATTHEW HENSON

1924–1955

A Heroine of the High Seas

American Louise Arner Boyd came from a wealthy family, which meant she could finance a number of sea expeditions to the north pole and Greenland. She helped document Greenland's fjords and glaciers by photographing them and, in 1955, was the first woman to fly over the north pole.

DOWN TO THE SOUTH POLE!

The discovery of the south pole was only possible via incredibly dangerous journeys across the infinite expanse of ice known as the Antarctic.

The south pole is located at one of the most isolated and inaccessible points of the Earth. Two competing teams—one British, the other Norwegian—set off simultaneously to try to reach it first.

1910–1912

The Race to the South Pole

Briton Robert Falcon Scott wanted to be a person who made history, and becoming the first to discover the south pole seemed like a great opportunity to achieve that. Meanwhile, the Norwegian Roald Amundsen had wanted to be the first to reach the north pole, but as Peary appeared to have already done so, Amundsen concentrated his efforts southward. The race was on ...

ROBERT FALCON SCOTT

When Scott and his crew reached the continent of Antarctica, they faced problems early on: the ponies they had brought along to pull their sleds were unable to walk on the ice and their motorized sleds soon broke down, which meant the men had to pull them themselves. This cost the team a great deal of energy and time.

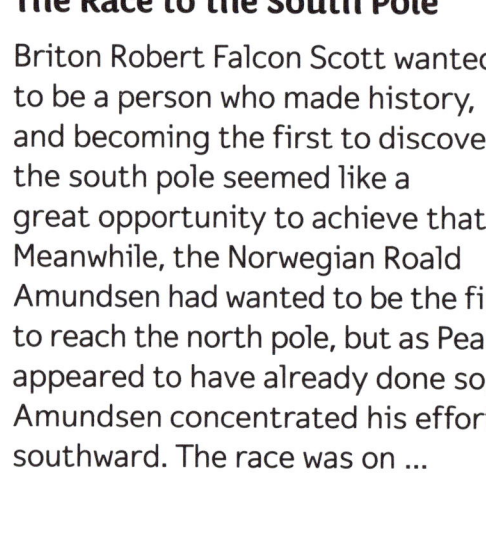

ROALD AMUNDSEN

South pole

Amundsen was the first to reach the south pole. Like Fridtjof Nansen, he used Inuit-style sleds. Scott's team still had a long way ahead of them at this point. When they finally reached the south pole, they were exhausted. On their return journey, they were engulfed by an ice storm, which led to their deaths. Although Amundsen won the race to the pole, Scott's diaries and the research efforts of his team were, and remain, of great importance.

Polynesians in the Antarctic

According to Polynesian legend, Ui-te-Rangiora is said to have discovered the Antarctic Ocean. Although Polynesians are unlikely to have reached the south pole, they did travel a great distance south, as recovered pottery remnants prove.

Emma, when do we go back to warmer weather?

Jackie Ronne

The American researcher Jackie Ronne was the first woman to be an active member of an Antarctic expedition. Her team spent a year on the continent conducting experiments. She would later return to Antarctica 15 times to carry out more research.

1931–1937

INGRID CHRISTENSEN

1946–1948

JACKIE RONNE

PENGUINS!

The First Female Polar Researcher

Ingrid Christensen was a Norwegian polar researcher who undertook four expeditions to Antarctica in the 1930s. She was not only the first woman to set foot on Antarctica, but also the first to fly over it.

On one major expedition to Antarctica, British polar researcher Ernest Shackleton's team and their ship got stuck in the ice, with the vessel eventually sinking. The outside world thought they had died, but Shackleton and some of the men eventually set off in rowboats in search of help. After a very difficult journey, they reached what is thought to have been a whaling station and the entire team was able to be rescued—four months after Shackleton had left them.

43

UP, UP, AND AWAY!

Humans have always dreamed of being able to fly. As early as antiquity and throughout the Middle Ages, all kinds of flying objects were conceived.

People look super tiny from above!

The First Attempts at Flight

In about 1500, the Italian painter and polymath Leonardo da Vinci created sketches that, for the era he was living in, were very advanced—the flight patterns of birds were even incorporated into his blueprints. However, these first drafts did not lead to human flight, and a successful attempt did not happen until the eighteenth century.

The Montgolfier brothers worked in their family business of paper manufacturing. Joseph-Michel Montgolfier, the elder of the two, became interested in making parachutes and once even jumped from the roof of the family house with one attached, a rather dangerous affair. He and his brother Jacques-Étienne discovered that heated air could cause a balloon to remain airborne and used wool- and hay-based fabric to capture as much hot air as possible. In June 1783 they succeeded in launching the first flight made by a hot-air balloon, which lasted 10 minutes and was unmanned.

Da Vinci's air propeller was based on the same principle as the modern helicopter. This technology was anything but new, however, as the Chinese had been using it for 2,500 years to make flying spinning tops for children.

The maiden journey (that is, the first journey of a new means of transportation) of the first powered airship took place in 1852. Its inventor, Henri Giffard, was one of the foremost experts when it came to steam power, and his airship traveled 17 miles (27 kilometers) from Paris to Trappes!

The debate to settle who actually achieved the first motorized flight took many years to be resolved. The Wright brothers' attempt was photographed in 1903. Two years earlier, however, newspapers had reported a successful attempt by a man named Gustav Weisskopf. Unfortunately, the images documenting this are blurred and difficult to interpret.

The First Transatlantic Flight

Charles Lindbergh dreamed of flying as a child, and as an adult this drive compelled him to become a pilot. He heard of a competition that promised USD 25,000 to the first person able to fly nonstop across the Atlantic. Many had failed to make the journey and a lot of people assumed Lindbergh would simply add to this list of failed aviators, but in 1927, 33 hours 30 minutes after his departure from New York, he landed in Paris. The crowd that greeted him was enthusiastic. But he wasn't actually the first to complete a transatlantic flight: eight years earlier, John Alcock and Arthur Brown flew from Newfoundland to Ireland, receiving little fanfare for their achievement.

1927

Lindbergh's plane was called the Spirit of St. Louis, but the press often referred to it as a "flying orange crate."

A Daredevil Pilot

Born toward the end of the nineteenth century, Bessie Coleman defied the prejudices of her time: she was the first African-American woman and Native American to gain an international pilot's license. She spent several years traveling around the U.S., performing dangerous stunts in her airplane for an admiring public.

1921

BESSIE COLEMAN

NR-7952

AMELIA EARHART

Coleman died during a test flight before an air show. Amelia Earhart is believed to have crashed while attempting to fly around the world—her airplane remains missing to this day.

1932

Flying Solo Across the Atlantic

The American pilot Amelia Earhart was the first woman to complete a solo flight across the Atlantic. She had already crossed the ocean in a plane before, but as a passenger. Her solo flight made her the first person to fly across the Atlantic twice.

ON TOP OF THE WORLD

Why do people climb enormous mountains? When mountaineer George Mallory was asked why he was attempting to scale Mount Everest, he famously replied: "Because it is there!" Let's climb up into the clouds and see what it is all about ...

For a long time, people tended to avoid mountains, as they were difficult to travel over and also very dangerous. In addition, there was little that could be grown on them.

Got you!

Mountains play an important role in many religious stories—Mount Olympus was said to be the home of the Greek gods, and in the Bible, mountains are described as symbolic of God's power.

In a letter, the fourteenth-century Italian poet Francesco Petrarch wrote about ascending Mont Ventoux in France. As a result, many consider him the father of mountaineering.

One of the greatest mountaineers is Italian Reinhold Messner. In 1986, he became the first person to have climbed all 14 of Earth's 26,250-feet (8,000-meter) peaks, and without the use of oxygen tanks.

In the eighteenth century, mountaineering was very popular. Clubs were founded in the mid-nineteenth century with the aim of exploring the Alps.

Why are we again in snowy weather?

Mount Everest

Located in the Himalaya mountain range in Asia—on the border between Nepal and Tibet, to be precise—Mount Everest is 29,029 feet (8,848 meters) high. At this altitude, the air is much "thinner," meaning that there is less oxygen, which makes breathing more difficult. These conditions have caused many expeditions to climb this mountain to fail. In 1924, the Englishmen George Mallory and Andrew Irvine died just before reaching its peak—or perhaps shortly afterwards. The fate of these two early summit-seekers remains unknown to this day.

New Zealander Edmund Hillary was 16 when he first discovered mountaineering. In 1952, he accepted an offer to take part in an expedition to climb Mount Everest. Among his companions when the team set out the following year was the Sherpa Tenzing Norgay. The Sherpa are a people from Nepal and well acquainted with the conditions climbers face in the Himalayas. Despite this, Norgay had previously tried to reach the world's highest summit with no success. This time he was going to make it!

Hillary and Norgay remained life-long friends and refused to say who had reached the summit first. They wanted to share the fame.

1953

TENZING NORGAY

EDMUND HILLARY

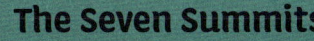

The way to the summit was long and exhausting. Nine camps were erected as the team made their way up the mountain—more than 400 people took part in the expedition overall, with 362 being there simply to help carry the 28,660 pounds (13,000 kilograms) of equipment. In addition, there were 20 Sherpas, who took over leadership of the team. Hillary and Norgay reached the summit of Everest on May 29, 1953.

The Seven Summits

The first woman to reach the summit of Mount Everest was Japanese climber Junko Tabei, in 1975. She also successfully reached all Seven Summits— the highest peaks on each of the world's seven continents.

JUNKO TABEI

THE MYSTERIOUS OCEAN DEEP

Life underwater remained a mystery to most for many years. It might be hard to believe, but two-thirds of our planet is actually water.

Underwater Gear

Conditions underwater are extremely demanding on the human body. In order to investigate life below the surface, a lot of high-tech equipment is required. The diver portrayed in this image is Jacques-Yves Cousteau, who invented the Aqua-Lung. Using this device along with air tanks allows people to stay underwater for much longer than normal. Any idea what other equipment you might need to go diving?

JACQUES-YVES COUSTEAU

from 1936

The diving bell has been in use since antiquity. When the bell is plunged underwater with the opening facing downwards, air remains trapped in the upper section. An air hose attached to this space then provides divers with atmospheric oxygen.

As early as 1797, inventor Karl Heinrich Klingert built a special diving suit with a helmet. Klingert was a prolific inventor who also created the first electric clock, as well as many devices to help the ill and disabled.

The first piece of equipment made for individual divers was a metal helmet that was supplied with breathing air via a hose that led to the surface. Unfortunately the helmet was very heavy and therefore not very practical.

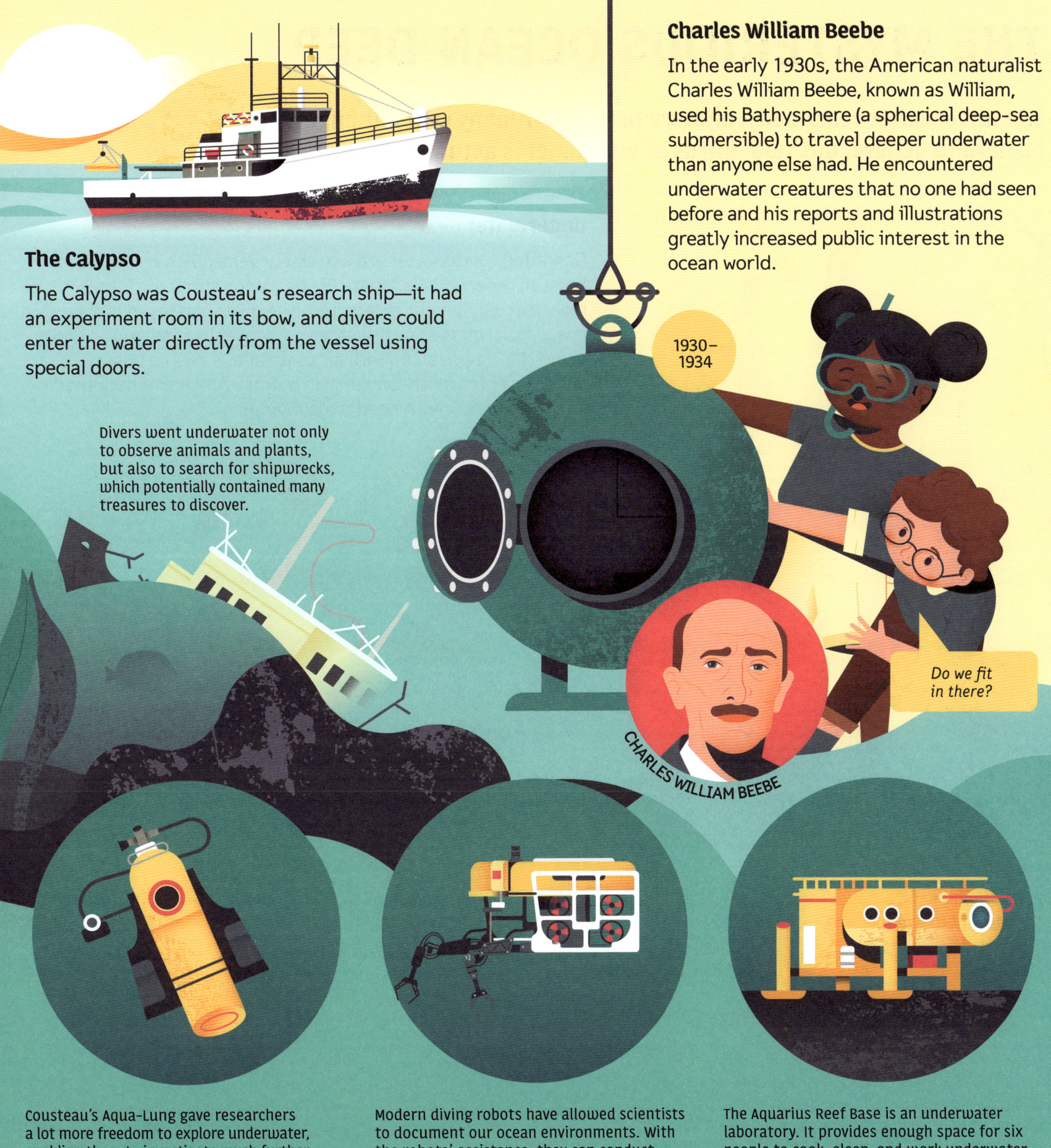

The Calypso

The Calypso was Cousteau's research ship—it had an experiment room in its bow, and divers could enter the water directly from the vessel using special doors.

Divers went underwater not only to observe animals and plants, but also to search for shipwrecks, which potentially contained many treasures to discover.

Charles William Beebe

In the early 1930s, the American naturalist Charles William Beebe, known as William, used his Bathysphere (a spherical deep-sea submersible) to travel deeper underwater than anyone else had. He encountered underwater creatures that no one had seen before and his reports and illustrations greatly increased public interest in the ocean world.

1930–1934

Do we fit in there?

CHARLES WILLIAM BEEBE

Cousteau's Aqua-Lung gave researchers a lot more freedom to explore underwater, enabling them to investigate much further and deeper than before and observe many animals and plants.

Modern diving robots have allowed scientists to document our ocean environments. With the robots' assistance, they can conduct underwater experiments without having to put themselves in danger.

The Aquarius Reef Base is an underwater laboratory. It provides enough space for six people to cook, sleep, and work underwater during missions that last 10 days on average.

HOT ON THE TRAIL OF HUMANITY

Where do we come from and how did we become who we are? The search to find the answers to these questions has long preoccupied many people who set off on journeys to discover more about the origins of our species.

1947

Thor Heyerdahl and the Kon-Tiki

Norwegian Thor Heyerdahl was greatly interested in the Polynesians. He believed that they originally came from South America. In order to prove his theory, he built a raft he named the Kon-Tiki, which he used to sail from South America across the Pacific Ocean. As a child, Heyerdahl was afraid of the water because he almost drowned twice, this meant that he refused to learn how to swim until he was in his early twenties. On his great journey in 1947, he spent 101 days on the ocean until he finally reached an island in Polynesia. Thus he felt he was able to prove that, more than 500 years previously (and possibly much earlier), people would have been capable of reaching Polynesia from South America.

Other researchers were skeptical of Heyerdahl's claims. Nowadays we know that he was partly correct: the Polynesians probably did not come from South America, but likely did have contact with indigenous South American peoples long before Columbus, perhaps trading with them. Remember what we were saying earlier about the sweet potato?

Did they bring the sweet potatoes on this raft?

During their journey, Heyerdahl and his team came across a seldom-seen whale shark.

THOR HEYERDAHL

Louis Leakey's Discovery

The British archaeologist Louis Leakey investigated several extinct species of apes. He led numerous archaeological digs in Africa in the mid-twentieth century that discovered the remains of humanity's oldest-known biological ancestors. This was the first conclusive evidence that humans had originated in Africa. Previously, it had been assumed that humans had originally come from Asia.

1931–1964

JANE GOODALL

We are the same size!

Jane Goodall

1960 until today

In the late 1950s, Leakey encouraged primatologist Jane Goodall, then working for him as his secretary, to conduct research with chimpanzees. She has spent more than 55 years living with them in the jungle and, in the process, discovered a myriad of important modes of behavior among the chimps—for example, that they use tools.

DIAN FOSSEY

1966–1985

Dian Fossey

Primatologist and conservationist Dian Fossey was also strongly influenced and supported by Leakey. She undertook an in-depth study of a group of mountain gorillas. Incredibly, they accepted her as one of their own and even entrusted her with their young, who played happily in her lap. She campaigned for the protection of gorillas, who remain at risk of extinction.

51

EXPLORING THE COSMOS

Stars, planets, infinite stretches of empty black space, and the question of whether there is life beyond Earth—the universe continues to hold great mystery for us humans.

The First Explorers of Space

The invention of rockets made the exploration of the extraterrestrial possible. The first journey into outer space was made by the Soviet Union (now called Russia) in 1957 with the launch of Sputnik 1, a satellite. It spent 92 days orbiting the Earth, measuring the temperature in space for the first three weeks. Soon after, living creatures were shot into space as well.

1961

Into the Void

Russian cosmonaut Yuri Gagarin came from a simple farming background before becoming world-famous as the first human to travel into space. In 1961, he flew around the world in 108 minutes in his spaceship, the Vostok 1.

A month after Sputnik 1 was launched, the small Russian dog Laika became the first dog to reach the Earth's orbit, but sadly lost her life during the flight. Two years later, two monkeys called Able and Baker, who were part of a U.S. mission, were the first living creatures to survive a return journey to Earth.

YURI GAGARIN

This is another journey around the world, but what happens if you get travel-sick up there?

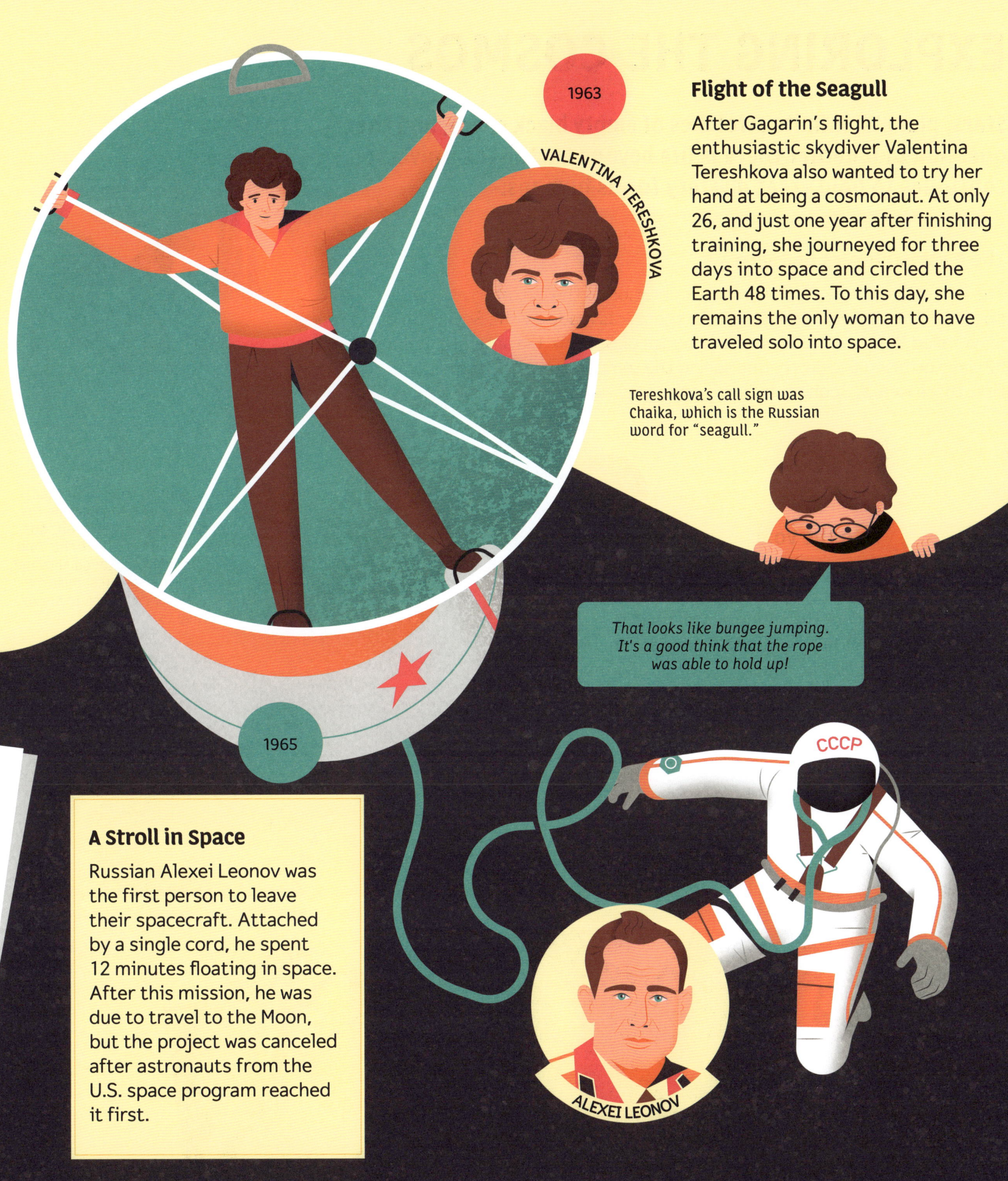

1963

VALENTINA TERESHKOVA

Flight of the Seagull

After Gagarin's flight, the enthusiastic skydiver Valentina Tereshkova also wanted to try her hand at being a cosmonaut. At only 26, and just one year after finishing training, she journeyed for three days into space and circled the Earth 48 times. To this day, she remains the only woman to have traveled solo into space.

Tereshkova's call sign was Chaika, which is the Russian word for "seagull."

That looks like bungee jumping. It's a good think that the rope was able to hold up!

1965

A Stroll in Space

Russian Alexei Leonov was the first person to leave their spacecraft. Attached by a single cord, he spent 12 minutes floating in space. After this mission, he was due to travel to the Moon, but the project was canceled after astronauts from the U.S. space program reached it first.

CCCP

ALEXEI LEONOV

Outer space became the stage for a battle for fame and power between the U.S. and the Soviet Union. Sputnik 1 and Gagarin had initially put the latter in the lead, but the U.S. struck back by being the first to land people on the Moon. In July 1969, the American astronauts Edwin "Buzz" Aldrin, Neil Armstrong, and Michael Collins arrived at their destination three days after takeoff, with Armstrong and Aldrin reaching the Moon's surface in a landing module while Collins stayed behind in the spaceship.

1969

EDWIN "BUZZ" ALDRIN

A TRIP TO THE MOON

NEIL ARMSTRONG

"That's one small step for a man, one giant leap for mankind," Armstrong said as he became the first person to set foot on the Moon, and indeed any heavenly body beyond Earth. At first, Armstrong and Aldrin had to get used to the Moon's conditions, such as low gravity and a slippery surface, then they could take samples and conduct tests before setting out on their return journey to Earth.

SPACE TRAVEL TODAY

Here in space it's all quite relaxed.

1998

This is the International Space Station, also known as the ISS—it is the largest human-made object to exist in space. After their fierce competition against one another in the space race, the U.S. and the Soviet Union eventually began cooperating on board the ISS. In total, 15 countries are part of the project.

Oh, I've got butterflies in my stomach!

The next desired destination in space is Mars. NASA, the U.S. government agency concerned with space travel and aeronautics, as well as a number of wealthy private citizens, want to reach it not only to conduct research but also to colonize it. Before this can become a reality, machines called Mars rovers are being used as the main tools to investigate conditions there. They take samples and go off on research trips of their own around the planet.

Whew, what a trip—through time, around the world, and even up into space! But after all the adventures that have already been undertaken, all the places that have already been found, and all the plants and animals that have already been described and recorded in books, are there still new things to be discovered?

There certainly are! There's still so much to be learned about the world around us. Researchers say that we have so far only discovered about 10 percent of the world's animal species, and that at least 90 percent of the oceans remain unexplored. Hard to believe, right? Many caves and mountains also remain completely foreign to us humans—and as for the infinite expanse of outer space …

There are probably more unclimbed than climbed mountains on Earth. For example, no one has yet reached the peak of Gangkhar Puensum, Bhutan's highest mountain at 24,836 feet (7,570 meters). Under the ice of the Antarctic, there are innumerable rivers and lakes that no human has ever laid eyes on, and that could contain new species, some of which will have remained separate from the rest of the world for 120,000 years because of the thick layers of ice.

Our planet is so incredible and diverse that, for many years into the future, we will continue to find new places and creatures that we can hardly begin to imagine today. But whenever we discover something previously unknown, the journeys that will take us there and, above all, the people we will meet along the way will provide us with totally new experiences.

So what are you waiting for? Adventure awaits!

Explore the World

Discoveries that shaped our world

by Anton Hallmann

This book was conceived, edited, and designed by Little Gestalten.

Edited by Robert Klanten and Maria-Elisabeth Niebius

Translation from German by Ryan Eyers

Design and layout by Anton Hallmann
Typefaces: Calcine by Mark Frömberg, Hellschreiber Sans by Jörg Schmitt

Printed by Nino Druck GmbH, Neustadt/Weinstraße
Made in Germany

Published by Little Gestalten, Berlin 2021
ISBN 978-3-96704-703-5

For more information, and to order books, please visit www.little.gestalten.com.

Bibliographic information published by the Deutsche Nationalbibliothek.
The Deutsche Nationalbibliothek lists this publication in the Deutsche Nationalbibliografie; detailed bibliographic data are available online at www.dnb.de.

This book was printed on paper certified according to the standards of the FSC®.

Anton Hallmann was born in Brandenburg and studied illustration at the Hamburg University of Applied Sciences. He is primarily working in editorial illustration for newspapers such as *Die Zeit, Süddeutsche Zeitung, FAZ,* and clients including Google, Lufthansa, and Deutsche Bahn. He currently lives in Stockholm.
Explore the World is his first children's book.